I0470400

Who Do You Say I Am?

Knowing Jesus, Understanding the Church, and Walking in Kingdom Authority

Doug Roberts

Who Do You Say I Am?

Knowing Jesus, Understanding the Church, and Walking in Kingdom Authority

by Doug Roberts

Copyright © 2017 Doug Roberts

Published by:

> *Doug Roberts Publishing*
> *P.O. Box 321*
> *Frederick, Oklahoma 73542*

Unless otherwise indicated, scripture quotations are taken from the New American Standard Bible® (NASB), Copyright © 1960, 1962, 1963, 1968, 1971, 1972, 1973, 1975, 1977, 1995 by The Lockman Foundation. Used by permission. www.Lockman.org

Scripture quotations marked MSG are taken from THE MESSAGE, copyright © 1993, 1994, 1995, 1996, 2000, 2001, 2002 by Eugene H. Peterson. Used by permission of NavPress. All rights reserved. Represented by Tyndale House Publishers, Inc.

Printed in the United States of America

ISBN: 978-0-9825992-2-8

I thank Ed Chinn, Tim and Laurie Thornton, Shellie Kushnerick and Fred White for all the work they did helping me transfer the things in my heart into print.

I want to say thank you to the most amazing woman, my wife Rita, who without my journey would have not been complete.

Table of Contents

Chapter 1: Who is Jesus?

Now when Jesus came into the district of Caesarea Philippi, He began asking His disciples, saying, "Who do people say that the Son of Man is?" And they said, "Some say John the Baptist; and others, Elijah; but still others, Jeremiah, or one of the prophets." He said to them, "But who do you say that I am?" And Simon Peter answered and said, "Thou art the Christ, the Son of the living God." And Jesus answered and said to him, "Blessed are you, Simon Barjona, because flesh and blood did not reveal this to you, but My Father who is in heaven. And I also say to you that you are Peter, and upon this rock I will build My church; and the gates of Hades shall not overpower it. I will give you the keys of the kingdom of heaven; and whatever you shall bind on earth shall be bound in heaven, and whatever you shall loose on earth shall be loosed in heaven."

— Matthew 16:13-19

Imagine this scenario. Here's Jesus with His disciples, asking, "What are the people saying about me here? Who do the people say that I am?" And Peter stands up and says, "Well, some say you're John the Baptist, others say you're Elijah, still others say you're Jeremiah or one of the prophets."

That is a very general description of what people were saying about Jesus, but Jesus goes on and says, "But, who do *you* say that I am?" Yes, He did want to know

Jesus is saying, "Peter, you didn't hear that from men. Your pastor didn't teach you that. You didn't read it from books. But my Father told you who I am."

what the people were saying about Him in that region, but quickly He comes down to the real issue: "But who am I to *you*?"

You Are The Christ, The Son Of The Living God

It's important to know who Jesus is. Peter stood up and said, "You are the Christ, the Son of the living God." I love how The Message phrases Jesus' response, "You didn't get that answer out of books or from teachers. My Father in heaven, God Himself, let you in on the secret of who I really am." (MSG)

Jesus is saying, "Peter, you didn't hear that from men. Your pastor didn't teach you that. You didn't read it from books. My Father told you who I am."

Now I'm going to tell you who you are

We need to be able to hear from the Father. Too many times we only hear from people and not from the Father. And see, Jesus said, "You've heard from my Father who I am." And He goes on to say, "Now that you've heard from my Father about Who I am, I'm going to tell you who *you* are." And then, "Now that you know who you are, all kingdom authority has been given to you."

And then Jesus went on to say, "You are Peter, a rock. This is the rock on which I will put together my church, a church so expansive with energy that not even the gates of hell will be able to keep it out. And that's not all. You will have complete and free access to God's kingdom, keys to open any and every door; no more barriers between heaven and earth, earth and heaven. A yes on earth will be a yes in heaven." (MSG)

Jesus says, "Now that you've heard from my Father and who my Father says that I am, *now I'm going to tell you who you are.*"

When you know who you are in Christ, then all kingdom authority has been given to you: "A yes on earth is a yes in heaven. A no on earth is a no in heaven." This is the authority that we have as believers when we know who Jesus is—when Jesus tells us who we are, then we can go with the kingdom authority to do what the Father has called us to do.

When Jesus tells us who we are, then we can go with the Kingdom authority to do what the Father has called us to do.

But see, some churches don't want people to be able to hear from the Father. They just want people to hear from the priest or pastor. They don't want people to read the Word, they don't want people to know who they are in Christ, they just want people to know what the church leaders tell them.

We'll return to the kingdom authority we have been given in a second, but first let's discover the truth about the Church.

Chapter 2: What is the Church?

First, the Church is not a *what*—She is a *who!* She is Jesus' bride!

I've been married for 43 years, and, let me tell you, I don't want any other man's handprints on my wife. I just want my handprints on her. Why? Because she's *my* wife.

Why would we think Jesus would want us to put our handprints on His bride? She—the Church—is *His bride*. We need to spend more time with Him, the groom, to find out what He wants His bride to become so that when the groom arrives, the bride will be fully prepared for him.

Unfortunately, we get trapped into thinking the bride is ours— that she belongs to us—just because we're the pastor or church leader.

How Many Churches?

Sometimes when I speak, I ask the audience, "How many churches are there in this city?" After hearing their responses, I remind them there is just one. We're all part

If you are the Church, how can you go to church?

of Christ's Church. Even though we meet in different places, there's just one Church. It's like a family. I don't live with my mother; she has her own house. My children don't live with me; they have their own house. But we're still just one family. Occasionally we all get together and celebrate together because we're family. The Church is the same way. There's just one Church, but there are many members in that Church. We've got to get our minds renewed. How many times do you get up on Sunday and say, "I've got to go to church!" Well, let me ask you a question: If you *are* the Church, how can you go to church?

Where any two or three come together, there is the Church. *We* are the Church. Wherever we go, there is the Church, but because we don't understand the heart of the Father, we don't understand what Jesus has commanded. We go out and build some great structure, call it "Church," and then tell people, "Come be part of my church."

The Church Is a Family

I don't want to be part of your church; I want to be part of your family. I'm in Jesus' Church and you're in Jesus' Church, so now we can have relationship and have fellowship. We're family! Why? Because God is our Father, Jesus is our brother, and that makes us family. We can and should act as family. Now, I know that

6

when we have family reunions there are some members of the family we hope don't come, but if they do come, they're still family.

Therefore, when we come into a place of being able to hear from the Father and the Father tells us who Jesus is, and Jesus tells us who we are, then we've been given kingdom authority to do what God has called us to do in Christ. When you hear from the Father, that "hearing" gives you faith to believe what the Father is saying. When you remain in that kind of relationship or love, you are considered a friend and not a servant.

My son is 40 years old. He's my son, but he's also my friend. I like just hanging out with him. You could ask my son how I'm going to respond to a situation and he can tell you because he knows me. Why? Because we spend time together. We have relationship together. We enjoy one another.

To many people, the only Jesus they're ever going to know is you.

We, the Church, are now God's expression on the earth. We should know the nature of the Father. We should know the compassion and the nature of Jesus. We should know the unconditional love that has been given to us. That is what we are to give to the earth.

To many people, the only Jesus they're ever going to know is you. The Psalmist said, "Taste and see and know that God is good." You're part of His body on the earth. How do you taste? Do you taste sweet? Or bitter? Do you taste loving? Or hateful? Do you taste gentle? Or harsh? Do you taste compassionate? Or are you a bitter, judgmental person? Taste and see and know that God is good. We must be the reflection of Him on the earth.

Chapter 3: How Can You Walk in His Authority?

Luke 10:19, says, "I have given you authority to tread on serpents and scorpions, and over all the power of the enemy; nothing shall injure you."

I may not be very smart, but when the Word says "all," I think that means *everything*. Is that right? He says, "I have given you authority over all." Does that leave out anything? No! You have authority as children of God in every area that God has placed you. Therefore, no weapon formed against you can prosper; no plan set against you can succeed. Why? Because if God is for you, who can be against you? This is who you are. Do you believe that?

Healing On Aisle 5

If we really believe this, then every place we go, others should see the kingdom of God being established. We should be looking for victims. I define a victim as someone

Are you looking for "victims?" I define a victim as someone who is getting ready to encounter the love of God.

who is getting ready to encounter the love of God. There is a need? Pray for them with belief and watch what God does. I challenge you—when you leave today, go look for your victims.

In Walmart you often hear something like this: "Aisle 7. Sale on aisle 7." What if God's people would go into Walmart, grab the intercom and say, "Healing on Aisle 5. If you need healing, if you need deliverance, if you need love, go to aisle 5. Let us pray for you."

This is who we are! I mean, think about it. As Jesus walked the streets, what happened? Kingdom happened. People got healed, people got saved, people got delivered, people were called into a new identity. Isn't that true? That's who we are. That's the authority that's been given to us. 1 John 4 tells us that as He is, so are we in this world.

But do we believe that?

Did You Go Or Were You Sent?

Let's look at what Luke 10:19 says in The Message. It says, "See what I've given you? Safe passage as you walk on snakes and scorpions, and protection from every assault of the Enemy. No one can put a hand on you. All the same, the great triumph is not in your authority over evil, but in God's authority over you and presence with you. Not what you do for God but what God does for you—that's the agenda for rejoicing."

Years ago a man named Reuben Odongo lived in Kenya, and he was going into Sudan for ministry. But when he got to the border, they beat, stripped him, and left him naked. Some of the brothers came and got him, and after a while Reuben realized that God had sent him to Sudan and he was not going to let the devil rob him of what God had called him to do.

So, he went back. When he got to the border, they came to attack him again. But this time he said, "No, stop! God has sent me here and you're not going to stop what God has called me to do," and they let him enter the country. Revival broke loose. People got saved. People got delivered. The kingdom was established. Why? Because he'd heard from the Father that God had sent him there and he knew that no weapon formed against him could prosper. He said, "I wished I had been listening earlier."

It's one thing to go; it's another thing to be sent. When you're building a ministry, you can go. When you're establishing the kingdom, you wait until you're sent. An invitation by itself doesn't mean anything, but when you hear "Go" from the Lord, you know you're being sent with all authority of the Father to do what God's called you to do. But when we don't know who we are in Christ, we're always looking for opportunities to exercise our gift, to exercise our ministry, so that people can see how great and how spiritual we are. That's all about us! But when it's about Christ in me, working though me, then the Father is glorified.

Chapter 4: Where is His Kingdom?

Sometimes people say, "I want to join your organization." And I say, "I don't have an organization. You're already in my family." I'm not against organizations. I have a name and title and all that stuff. But our fellowship is not in organization; it's in relationship.

I sometimes don't even know what a brother or sister believes. And they often don't know what I believe. Our fellowship is not in doctrine; our fellowship is in Christ.

Sometimes I disagree with my own doctrine. Have you ever had to change your doctrine? Because the more revelation I get, I sometimes realize, *man, that was stupid!* I only know one man who has 100% pure doctrine, and that's Jesus. The rest of us are in a learning process. That's why we need relationship. I can't do what others do, so I don't try. And others can't do what I do. And most of them don't try. There's no competition in the family of God. There's no jealousy in the family of God. At least there shouldn't be.

Can We Get Beyond Our Doctrine?

You know what gives me more joy than anything? If I leave a place after a time of ministry and the people begin doing things they weren't doing when I came. If they're more like Jesus after I leave than before I came. I don't even care if they remember my name. But do they remember Jesus? Do they remember what He's called them to do?

I've heard leaders and pastors tell me, "Brother Doug, I see that in the Bible, but it's not our doctrine."

Always remember who you are in Him. Do the works that Jesus called you to do.

I've heard leaders and pastors tell me, "Brother Doug, I see that in the Bible, but it's not our doctrine."

You know what I tell them? I say, "Well, where did you learn your doctrine?"

"Oh, Grandma taught us the doctrine."

"Well, where's your grandma at now?"

"She's dead."

"Oh, so you're consulting with the dead instead of listening to the living? That's witchcraft."

Where In The World Is Your Kingdom, Lord?

Righteousness, peace, and joy are fruits of the Spirit which the Father gives us when we yield to His will in our lives. Some people say, "Well, the kingdom of God *is* righteousness, peace, and joy in the Holy Spirit." No, that's not the kingdom of God. That's the *fruit* of living in the kingdom of God. When you're living in the kingdom of God, you have righteousness, you have peace, and you have joy. Why? Because you're living in God's rule and reign and sovereignty. The kingdom of God is God's rule, God's authority, God's presence.

That's why you can't say, "Well, there is the kingdom, or the kingdom is over there." The kingdom is in us. Why? Because the King lives in us. So wherever we set our foot, there is the kingdom of God. Why? Because I'm here. Because you're there. Because the kingdom lives within us.

So as you go believing—believing what God has said about you in Christ; believing what Jesus has called you to do—then all kingdom authority is given to you. A yes on earth is a yes in heaven.

Why is this so? Because you're His ambassador, representing Him on the earth, and you are to do what He's called you to do. You are not called to do what you want to do, but to do what He's called you to do.

I believe that each one of us is going to give an account before the Father for what He's predestined us to do in Christ. We will not have to give an account for what we did, but for how obedient we were in doing what He called us to do. If God called you to be a banker and to be His representative in the marketplace and you quit being a banker because you want to be a pastor, you're in sin. If God called you to be a teacher in the public schools and you do something else, you're in sin. If God called you to be a pastor and you try to do something else, you're in sin. That's why it's important to hear from the Father to know what He is telling you about Jesus, and then for Jesus to be able to tell you who we are.

That is the essence of the Kingdom of God—doing what He says!

Chapter 5: Where is Your Identity?

I've been in the ministry now for 43 years, but I don't pastor a church. I'm a son. As a son, I pastor my Father's people. I own nothing, but I have a lot of things. Why? Because God has entrusted me with the work that He's called me to do.

I minister in Spain, Mexico, Germany, Africa, Argentina, Chile, Canada, Mongolia, China, and in the United States, but I don't have a ministry. I'm just a son. My identity is as a son. So it doesn't bother me if you don't like what I do because I'm not trying to please you. I'm trying to please the One who sent me.

What are the two worst things you can do to me?

My identity is as a son. So it doesn't bother me if you don't like what I do, because I'm not trying to please you. I'm trying to please the One who sent me.

1. Kill me? If you kill me, I'm in the presence of the Lord. Not a bad thing.

2. Not invite me to minister? If you don't invite me to be with your people I get to stay home, play a little golf, and enjoy my family. Not a bad thing.

So the two worst things you can do to me are both great blessings for me!

We don't fear men; we fear the Lord. And we don't please men; we please the Lord. Now, Jesus was pleasing to the Father. But who killed Him? Religious people. So now you have a problem. Do you want to please religious people? Or do you want to please God and be killed by religious people?

Freedom!

What sets people free? The truth! When you know the truth and apply the truth it will set you free. As leaders and pastors, we need to be teaching truth, not traditions of men. Hopefully our traditions have truth in them, but there's no place in Scripture where Jesus said, "Go preach your traditions." He said, "Go therefore and make disciples of all the nations, baptizing them in the name of the Father and the Son and the Holy Spirit, teaching them to observe all that I commanded you…" (Matt. 28:19-20).

People are not my source. A job is not my source. My ministry is not my source. God is my source. I can only teach that which I've been taught. I can only teach the revelation that God has given me because that is what makes me who I am. I'm not a professional minister; I'm a son. My ministry flows from my identity. If you cut me, I'll bleed what I'm teaching because I believe what I am saying. But my ministry is not my source and it isn't my identity. God, my Father, has proven Himself to me for 43 years. People are not my source. A job is not my source. My ministry is not my source. God is my source.

The Problem with Identistry

Do you know what "identistry" means? I created the word—it describes what happens when someone gets their identity from their ministry. In other words, it's when someone has to have a ministry in order to know who they are. But the truth is, our identity is in Christ. and because our identity is in Christ, then we have a ministry.

The focus is not the ministry, the focus is Christ and hearing who Christ is because God has predestined you for good works in Christ. Where are those good works? Are they in your ministry or are they in Christ? God has predestined you to do good works *in Christ*. So if you're outside of Christ, I don't care how good it is— it's still sin. But if you're in Christ, I don't care how bad a job you do, God's going to bless it because you're walking in faith.

I have a word for a lot of people in and out of ministry: Get a job! Because if God has called you in the marketplace He has a congregation there for you

Our religious concepts so often limit how much we can even see the Kingdom of God.

to teach and that will be where you fill up who you are in Christ. A preacher might not ever have access to that congregation. I pastor men who are not full-time pastors. Why? Because they're apostles or prophets in the marketplace. See? The gifts of God are not limited to a meeting in a building we call church.

Our religious concepts often limit how much we can even see the kingdom of God. We need to change our minds about these things. For example, some of you are pastors, but you'll never have a congregation that meets in a building. Some might ask, "How can I be a pastor when I don't have a building?" I say, your identity is not in a building—your identity is in Christ with the people that He entrusted to you, so get a job so He can bless you in what and where He called you to do.

For 43 years I've never called anyone and asked, "Can I come preach for you? Years ago I told the Lord, "God this is your deal." I said, "If you want me to go, I'll go. But if you know how many hairs I have on my head then you also have my phone number. If you want me to go someplace, you have people call me." So I go, not because I want to but because God sends me. There are places I go that I wish I didn't have to go. But I don't have a choice, because God sent me. He loves the people.

When I go, I go as an ambassador, equipping people in their identity in Christ to do the work that God called them to do.

That's what it's about: *you* doing the work. Teaching people how to do the work. Calling people into their purpose in Christ. Calling people into their destiny in Christ. It's not about building a church.

Jesus said, "I will build my Church."

We are not supposed to build a church. He called us to make disciples.

He's equipping you to do the work, and the only way you can do it is to know your identity in Him.

Chapter 6: Who Pays For The Ministry?

Let's look at what Luke 12:32 says, "Do not be afraid, your Father has chosen gladly to give you the kingdom." Do we believe that? Do we really believe that God wants to give us His kingdom? I think we all know that sometimes we don't really believe it.

When I preached in Mexico a little while ago, I held up a $20 bill and said, "It would give me joy to give this to you. It would make me happy to give this to you." Someone came right up and grabbed it, and that gave me joy!

If giving away $20 pleased me, then how much more does it please the Father to give us His kingdom? But too often we don't believe that he wants to or that it would please him if we came up and took it. If I offered you a $20 bill and you didn't believe I wanted to give it away, you would miss out on a blessing because you didn't believe what I was saying. We so often miss out on what God has for us because we don't believe what He says. Religion teaches us to look at the free gift of the kingdom and mumble something like, "It's not our doctrine. It's not our tradition. We

Even though the check was made out to me, it was not my $10,000.

have never done that before." But when we do that, we miss out! It really does please the Father to give His children things in Christ.

Where are God's blessings for you? In Christ. Where do you live? In Christ! So, you live where God's blessings are! Do you believe that? If you believed it, you'd be living differently.

Whose Money Is It?

Years ago when I was planning to go to Mongolia, the Lord spoke to me: "I want you to take $10,000 to Mongolia." I said okay even though I didn't have that kind of money. But I said yes.

I told my wife, "I'm going to take $10,000 to Mongolia."

She smiled and said, "Yeah, okay." When I went to the post office the next day I opened up my box, and there was a check for $10,000. It was made out to me, but it was not my $10,000. It was to take to Mongolia. I brought it home and showed it to Rita.

And she said, "Well, yeah, you've got to take that to Mongolia."

Here's another story. Once when I was planning to go to Argentina, the pastor who was my host also wanted me to go to Ushuaia, which is at the southern tip of Argentina. I asked, "How much will it cost?"

He said, "$1,000."

I said, "Well, we'll see."

As soon as I hung up the phone, I heard a knock at the door. The woman standing there told me, "The Father has blessed us and we want to bless you." And she gave me a check for $1,000. So I picked up the phone, called the pastor in Argentina, and said, "We're going to Ushuaia."

God finances His kingdom. For 43 years, I've never gone into debt in the ministry. I've said yes, and then when the money came in, I knew I was supposed to do what God called me to do. I don't finance God's kingdom. It's His. Too many leaders and pastors think they are supposed to finance their own ministry.

Who Is Your Real Provision?

I once worked with four different pastors in Mexico, and each one of them had a very small congregation—25 or 30 people.

Each one of them also had a building. And they each wanted me to come and minister to their people.

So I said, "I have an idea. Why don't all four of you come together and use one building?" It got quiet and I continued: "Are you afraid that you won't have any money? Are you afraid that one of the other pastors will get your money? Are you afraid you won't have an identity—that if you don't have a building with your name on it they won't know you're a pastor? Let's have one meeting where we'll have all four pastors. And when people come up, they can put their tithes in the bucket of the one that's watching for their soul."

All four of them just kind of muttered, "Well, I don't know."

I said, "Oh, so the reason that you don't want to come together and have one building is that you can't trust the Lord for your finances. So you're motivated by money more than you're motivated by the Spirit of God."

You see, I'm trying to teach you that people are not your provision. God is your provision.

One time I led a very wealthy family to the Lord. I prayed for them, and they got baptized in the Holy Spirit and their children went through deliverance. The Lord transformed their lives, and they gave me $50. After very similar ministry with another wealthy family, that family gave me $500.

So one day I was complaining to the Lord and told him I didn't think it was right. And He said, "What are you complaining about?"

"Well, one of those families gave me $50, and the other gave me $500."

And God said, " Do you have a need?

"No."

And He said, "Why do you need money?"

"Oh."

A couple months later, I went to the post office and saw a check in my box. I opened it up and said, "God, what is this?"

And He said, "You have a need."

Blessed Are The Poor

Matthew 6 tells us not to worry about what we will eat or drink. We should not worry about what we will wear. God knows we have need of those things. Instead, we are to seek first the kingdom of God and all these things will be added to us. But what often happens is that we go seeking the things. So, if I'm a pastor and you have money, I'd be tempted to say, "Brother, come and join my ministry! I'll make you an elder! I'll give you a high place!"

I went to the post office and saw a check in my box. I opened it up and said, "God, what is this?" And He said, "You have a need."

The truth is, sometimes rich people make poor leaders. Too many just don't understand the kingdom of God. I've seen men that came out of true poverty—out of the drug culture or out of being drunks and fighters in the world—and then came into an understanding of Jesus' love for them. They came into an understanding of the Father's kingdom. They're multi-millionaires today, and they're givers. But why? Because their identity is not in their money; their identity is in Christ and they know God is just trusting them to steward *His* money.

You can't out-give God. I've tried. No matter how much you give away, He gives more.

We were in a difficult financial place one time. Money was very tight, and we had some bills we couldn't pay. Our pastor brought in a preacher to minister to us. I didn't like the preacher; I didn't agree with what he was saying.

When it came time for the offering, the pastor said, "Let's pray. Ask God what He wants you to give."

Since I didn't like the guy, I wasn't going to give much. Besides, I didn't have much. But when I turned to Rita, she said, "I think we're to give him all the money we have in our checking account."

I thought, *I rebuke you, devil!* But the Lord said, "That's what I want you to do."

So my wife wrote a check while I sat there complaining about it: "God, I don't like this guy. I don't agree with his doctrine."

God said, "It doesn't matter. I like him."

So we gave away our money. Within a week, we had paid all our bills and we had more money in our bank account than what we gave away.

We heard from the Father, we obeyed what He said, and then God obligated Himself to do what He said.

Now, let me warn you—only do that if you hear from the Father. Just because God spoke it to me, doesn't mean you need to do that. I know a minister who said that God told him to give his car to a missionary. So he did, and within a day or two another man had given him a brand-new car. He shared that story with some Bible students, and several of them gave their cars away. Of course, they didn't do it because God told them to do it but because they wanted a new car. So, after giving their cars away, they had to walk.

Don't do something because someone else did it; do it because you hear from the Father. Faith comes by

There have been times when the Father told me to do things that were foolish to the world. But when I did what the Father said, His blessings came. Why? Because the Father said.

hearing, and hearing comes by the Word. When you hear from the Father, then the Father does what He says.

There have been times when the Father told me to do things that were foolish to the world. But when I did what the Father said,

His blessings came. Why? Because the Father said it. Not because my pastor said it. Not because I saw it on TV. Not because I read it in a book. But because I heard it from my Father.

If you are a leader or a pastor, your number one job is to bring people to completion in Christ—that they know who Jesus is, that they know who they are in Christ. Your job is not to build a ministry. Ministry is going to happen, but ministry must not be what motivates you. Hearing the Lord should be your motivation.

Chapter 7: How Can You Fulfill Your Destiny?

It's not about you; it's about the One in you. It's not about how great you are; it's about how awesome He is. It's not about what you do; it's about what He wants to do through you.

James 1:22-25 tells us, "But prove yourselves doers of the word, and not merely hearers who delude themselves. For if anyone is a hearer of the word and not a doer, he is like a man who looks at his natural face in a mirror, for once he has looked at himself and gone away, he has immediately forgotten what kind of person he was. But one who looks intently at the

Do you feel like you have a ministry of healing? Go start praying for the sick. Do you feel like you have a ministry of encouragement? Go start encouraging people.

perfect law, the law of liberty, and abides by it, not having become a forgetful hearer but an effectual doer, this man will be blessed in what he does."

James tells us to prove ourselves to be doers of the word and not just hearers. So many times we hear something and because we heard it, we think that's who we are. However, if you're not *doing* what you heard, you're deceiving yourself, and a deceiver is not going to get the blessing of the Lord.

Do The Ministry

If you've already believed in Christ, then start being in Christ. And be a doer of what you believe. Walk through the doors the Lord opens and see if His anointing is on what you are doing. Do you feel like you have a ministry of healing? Go start praying for the sick. Do you feel like you have a ministry of encouragement? Go start encouraging people. Do you feel like you have the gift of a teacher? Start teaching people. You're a son, you're a daughter, and you do things because of that.

The worst you can do in Christ is amazing! The best you can do in your flesh is sin. Because you're a spirit being, your flesh is dead. Come alive to your spirit. Some try to build ministries out of their flesh and out of their personalities instead of out of hearing what God says. Then what you end up with is a dead work.

Are You Building A Spider Web?

We're not building anything; we're just being who God has called us to be in Christ. We're making disciples, we're bringing everyone complete into Christ, we're raising them up to be leaders to go *do* the work that God's called them to do.

We're certainly not building a spider web. When a spider builds a big web, everything in that web is for one purpose: to feed the spider. The spider kills any other spider that comes into the web because he doesn't want any other spider to have his provision. Of course, what's sad is that too often the world looks at the Church and sees spider webs instead of the family of God.

The kingdom of God is about family and about discipling and about training up men and **Too often the world looks at the Church and sees spider webs instead of the family of God.** women to do greater things than you've done. Isn't that the heart of a father? For his sons and daughters to do greater things than he's done? Jesus said, "My desire is for you to do the works I did, and yet even greater works, because I go to the Father."

The real Church—Christ's body in the earth—is full of leaders who refuse to build spider webs. Instead they say, "Brother, come to our gathering. Bless my people. Help my people be who God's called them to be in Christ. Teach the things that you're teaching." That's the true heart of a father. He's not afraid that someone is going to steal his people. He walks open-handedly with the things God's given him. That's a true father.

The Hidden Agenda

True fathers in the Lord have a hidden agenda. They want you to be fully equipped in Christ and for you to fulfill your destiny in Christ.

If that kind of leader sees God raising you up, he says, "Hey, start a home group at your house. Be who God's called you to be." Or, "Hey, go to this city, and do what God's called you to do. If you need help I'll help you, but you're fully equipped." That's the true marking of a father.

And that is how God's people step into their destiny.

This has to be the heart of pastors and leaders—to see their people fulfill their destiny. You're building one thing: an altar where people can come and die. After they die, they are resurrected; they come alive in Christ.

Come follow me as I die. Take up your cross daily, deny yourself. Follow the One who has called you. This is who we are. And we can only fulfill our destiny if we're willing to die to ourselves.

I want to conclude this little book with three questions. Ask them in order and write down the answers:

1. Who is Jesus to you?
2. Who does Jesus say that you are?
3. What has the Father called you to do on the earth in Christ?

If you're part of a spiritual family please take those questions to your pastor. Tell him who Jesus is to you, who Jesus says you are, and what the Father has called you to do. Then allow him to help you fulfill that destiny.

When my son was born we dedicated him to the Lord. Prophetic words came forth that he was going to be prophetic and a teacher. Some said he would have the heart of a pastor. He was just a baby, and obviously there was a need for some training. Today, he's 40 years old—he prophesies, he teaches, he pastors. But when he was a baby, I didn't say, "Go do that!" He had to be formed through a process.

Tell your pastor, "This is who Jesus is to me. This is who Jesus says I am. And this is what the Father has called me to do." And then allow him to help you fulfill that destiny.

Some of the things God is speaking to you now might be in preparation for where He's calling you, but you need some discipling, some training, some help to get there. But that's the goal. In Isaiah, God said, "I am God, I declare the end before the beginning." God speaks our destiny to us and then we start. That's why we need accountability, that's why we need relationships, that's why we need someone speaking into our lives—to help us fill the purpose of what God is calling us to.

Group Discussion Guide

My hope and purpose for this book is to see it become seed in the rich soil of human hearts. These questions were put together by some brothers and sisters to help you work these truths into your life.

1. In Matthew 16: 13-19, Jesus asked His disciples, "Who do people say I am?" Peter blurted out, "You are the Christ, the Son of the Living God! When Jesus heard Peter's answer, He said, "You didn't get that answer out of books or from teachers. My Father in heaven, God Himself, let you in on the secret of who I really am." (MSG)

   Think about the difference between getting an answer from a book or a teacher or getting it directly from the Lord. What difference does it make?

   Recall a time when you knew you heard directly from the Lord. Did that make a difference in your life? Did that give you a new confidence in your faith walk?

2. What do you think Jesus meant when He said, "Whatever you shall bind on earth shall be bound in heaven, and whatever you shall loose on earth shall be loosed in heaven?"

   Have you experienced that binding/loosing in your own life?

3. We know that the Church is the bride of Christ, but how much do you really understand that He takes her very personally?

Do you think people can be too presumptuous with His bride? Do you see her primarily as a means of employment, courtship, or as a space for selling your products? How can you be more careful and respectful when you're around the bride of Jesus?

4. Why is it so much easier for most people to think of church as a building rather than as a family?

    What are some practical ways that we can begin to think differently about the nature of the Church?

    Have you ever experienced a true revelation about the familial nature of the Church? Talk about that with others.

5. We've all heard stories of new Christians (or even denominations) that tend to be presumptuous about handing snakes or other dangers animals or objects. Yet, Jesus did say in Luke 10:19 that He has given us authority to tread on serpents and scorpions, and over all the power of the enemy. He said that "nothing shall injure you."

    How can we walk in confidence rather than presumption? What difference does the Father's authority make in such situations? Have you ever ventured out when He didn't authorize you to do so? What was the result?

6. How would you describe or define the kingdom of God? How does it change your definition to know that "government" is a synonym for "kingdom"?

Romans 14:17 tells us that "the kingdom of God is...righteousness, peace, and joy." What does that mean to you?

Are you an ambassador for Christ in your workplace? What does that mean? Do you think of your job (in a factory, a school, a bank, etc.) as a career or a calling?

If it is a calling, how can you obey the One who called you?

7. What does "identistry" mean? What makes it such a powerful force in our lives? How can you you stop its hold on you and turn away from it?

8. When you have heard the Lord say "go" and you have responded "yes," how have you seen the Lord release the finances to accomplish his mission?

Have you ever tried to finance God's kingdom when the call or the timing wasn't from God? What was the result?

9. Has the Lord ever directed you to do something that seemed foolish? What did you do? What happened?

10. Talk about a time you stepped out to do what you believe and saw the Lord's anointing. It is time to be a doer in another area of your life?

11. What is the difference between the kingdom of God and a spider web?

Have you ever been caught in a religious spider web? Have you ever helped to build one?

12. Finally, take some time now to think about the three questions down from Matthew 16. Although they are personal, it is very helpful to discuss them with others.

Who is Jesus to you?

Who does Jesus say that you are?

What has the Father called you to do on the earth in Christ?